BLIZZARDS IN THE DESERT
An Anthology of Unorthodox Poems
Volume 1

By Donald Charles

Donald Charles
Donald Charles USA, 829 Franklin St., Gretna, LA, 70053

Copyright © Blizzards in the Desert - An Anthology of Unorthodox Poems - Vol. 1

No part of this publication may be reproduced electronically, mechanically, digitally or otherwise, without written permission.

DEDICATION

To all poetry lovers around the globe, especially those of you who have chosen to journey with me through volume 1 of Blizzards in the Desert.

To Angela, Tramaine, Trinity, Dalanie, and everyone else, in recognition of your individual and collective positive impact and inspiration you have had on my existence.

Rest In Peace, Rodney Spotville(Big Rodney), Andrew Jackson(Drew), Nelson Waits(Hawk), Kayla New

Peace and Blessing to All

THE HIDDEN LESSON

Cloudy visions of reality gradually stabbing me as I ride on this ever gliding dream
Eyes closed to those that oppose
Words can mean so much when motivated by the touch of temptation
As I descend like rain water, or ten thousand tears of 12 pain ridden fathers
Motherless or some other shit
The father, the brother, the sister, the mother sick with left, right, up, down ways to get around
Lost in time, feeling focused but living blind
Now I redesign the design of all the lost time on the dream that forever glides
Analyzing the message within the tears I learned of one-hundred and twenty thousand fears
So tired of moving reckless
God please give me the strength to manifest my destiny through my blessings
Plenty cries, no lies, and eleven more time answered questions
                        Part 1 of many, the hidden lesson

MANY DAYS HAVE FALLEN

Reacting to such a sweet song, it's the morning
Sunrise alone sets the tone
Beaten and bruised, used and abused like a worn down tool
Lord knows how we keep marching, continuing down such a dark road
Detour ahead but instead you move towards your destination
Face it, you would have reached it if it wasn't for hesitation
Times a wasting
Some say blessings come with patience so I'm happy I'm still here
No room for fear
Too much anxiety
Too much depression
Too much bullshit
Too many distractions to fear anything this journey has to offer
Haven't I eaten of the devil's pie
Why would I want more
Hopefully grace is in store
As I close this door of uncertainty, I walk as if I hold my days up
As those that have fallen blemish my path
Serious thinker, every step is a new concept
No regret for the past even though it kicked my ass
Many days have fallen
Many suns have yet to rise
I will proceed and give my all in my procession
Testimonies, no confessions
Evaded prison but lost vision
Soaked in the rain, burned by the heat
Paid the price to be nice, seems like such a rip-off
My heart is filled with humbleness, about ready to explode
My face reflects the mileage gained on this road
Many days have fallen, many nights have zoomed pass
In the day that I arrive at destination elsewhere, my only words will be
                                                  At last

A POEM CALLED INSOMNIA

4 o'clock in the morning and my kidney is bothering me
The television is radiating some weird programming in the background
So far I'm just grateful to be so me
I've fulfilled one of my callings, to find myself at the deepest most inner-core of my being
My eyes are open, 1, 2, and 3
I will always see
Dreams of meaning
Writer's block
Doors locked
My soul tells my mind to stay awake, while my mind is tired from unnecessary work
My side still hurts
My mind misreads my souls instruction in trying times
Felony crimes haunt me, reason being unseen
Dr. King envisioned the dream
Government funded laboratory research scientists plotted the scheme
Black roses in the concrete soaked in the cream
While you hide it, I can't deny it
My relationships are strained
I've lost more than I've gained
The chains my brother
Wake up before you hang yourself while you're asleep
                In the meantime I'll be up looking out for you and me

YOU'RE GUILTY

Pure divinity is what your aura spoke to me
To describe this feeling musically, you're my sweet symphony
Day one until infinity
My light in the darkest night
The residue of your love is what guides me home
But before I go into the depths of those details, let me explain to you that of which you are guilty of
My love
My love pay close attention to the reason you've been apprehended
Was it your intent to commit this criminal offence?
Well this is why I plead the case that you shall spend the rest of your adult life with me
I don't believe your crimes were accidental or coincidental
Your moves were carefully calculated, never to be underestimated
From day 1 until infinity, my attention has and always will be a victim of abduction by the natural essence of your God given energy
One shot one kill, you did that with your looks
Manipulated me with your creativity
Suffocated me with your love and held me captive with your mental stability
Deceptive sexual agility
No limit to your murderous ability
In my heart of hearts I noticed it from the beginning, the start
Inevitability is the focus of this chapter
Two souls loving in love
Real life no actors
I'm not that innocent, maybe I needed to be captured
I let it happen
It actually came to me in a dream
I mean, I mean your smile, your smell, your attitude, your hair
Your stare, your blink, your kiss, your wink
The nose, the face, the toes, the waist
Smooth criminal
Straight and direct, no subliminals
Straight murder, no breaks or intervals
I saw it coming and please believe me that I was and still am too much of a soulja to run from it
Fuck it, you know me, put the pedal to the metal and gun it
I'm a dreamer and I'm not scared to let my dreams define me
Now say this for me, "Let's Ride Clyde"
As I say in return, "Let's Roll Bonnie"
My dreamgirl welcome to my reality
Let's let destiny manifest
From day one until infinity, you're my lover, my lady, my wisdom, my world, my girl, my friend, my partner in crime until the end
These are your charges

How do you plead?

WHISPERS & SCREAMS

Whispers and screams
T-shirts and blue jeans
Hard days and bad dreams
Nightmares
Confused faces, lost races
Lady justice throwing cases
Paper chasing
I hear the screams
Lady liberty is ashamed
Just ask her, her answer will be whispered
I feel the screams
I hear the pain
Whispers and screams
                                        Who's to blame

DEAR STARS

Dear stars way up in the sky
Seen because you shine
Since I tend to admire you I need to get high so I can see eye to eye with you
Depending on your shine hoping my dreams come true
Selfish of me right
You were there through all the lonely nights and late flights
Before and after life
Even the death of Christ couldn't bring you down
You seem so still while the Earth just spins around and spins around
Star I wish I could hold you and mold you
Don't want to control you, just show you
Some of the shit that I go through
Supposedly we're suppose to be controlled by this force called gravity that's constantly grabbing me
I prayed to you once again last night hoping that you share your light
And found out that the sun lights up the night
So starting tomorrow it'll be the sun that I pray to
Not that I hate you
I just love the one that illuminates you
So I thank you
For helping me see the light
                        One love to the stars whom shine bright at night

NOW BOARDING

Can you smell the grass through the glass
Vivid imagination while you're waiting
True friends vouch for your reasoning
I must go
The plane is boarding
No definite answer to where it is I'm going
To touch a cloud I surely will
A small piece of heaven, I hope it can heal
I'm off to see myself from the inside out
Above the world I left behind
Who knows what I'll find out
People get ready we're about to take flight
Singing songs of freedom aboard this flight

THE HANDS OF TIME

No situation is the same so feelings get distorted in the midst of the oceans healing
Wishing that waves would rise to the ceiling to wash away all decay
The ocean spray feels good to the new generation
Green to the undiscovered truths of fornication
No retribution, just confusion
No reciprocity, just hypocrisy
Silence cries in the deep blue sky
Depression is depressed through the magnetism of human flesh
So all things shall change with the coming of a new age
New blood to replace the poisoned
Before freedom and democracy we shall create a new world order
Peace unto the masses
The funnel of time is clear
The tunnel of life is near
Old things get washed away, like fear
Fear of flying
Fear of trying
Fear of dying
Time to find our way as we walk through sands of an hour glass in God's hands
Strong shall we forever stand

ANISHA'S PERFECTION

Let me explain perfection
Perfection is you
It's your challenging intellect
My reflection in your eyes
This is perfection at its peak
You plus me
I hate science but I love our chemistry
I envision myself sailing in your sea
Getting swallowed up in your ocean
Intoxicating myself with your potion
With you I share my portion
Perfection is your hairstyle
It's your beautiful smile that brightens up my day more than a sunrise with no clouds
It's your voice, your words of choice
It's your laser beam eyes penetrating my soul and mind
A second of touching you is a lifetime of loving you
A minute of holding you is the sweetest 60 seconds unknown to every other man besides me
You are my perfection
This is my confession
It's your sexy smell
Your painted fingernails
It's your ambition
Your drive
Your lips
Your thighs
Let me feel your soul and taste your thoughts
Let me smell your love as I speak and listen to your heart
Let me see your destiny
Time doesn't exist when you're next to me
So I'll keep it short and sweet because I would hate to believe that I bore you
        Just wanted to let you know that I respect, admire, and adore you

LOVERS 4 LIFE

Three times a lady, let me prove it to you tonight
As we steal away a slow moment from such a fast world
This is for all the girls who give romance a chance
Did his thug appeal seal the deal
Were you surprised by the modesty in his eyes
Let's love
As our minds connect, our bodies will follow and take lead
Take heed to the experienced and learn that ecstasy can be achieved
Listen to the breathing patterns
Smell the compatibility
Eat of the fruit of the sweetest taboo
See that the borders of our intimacy at this time are outside the realms of reality and unreachable in the midst of our love
Mind moving slower and more steady than the hands of time
As my hands mold the sand within your hourglass
Taking it slow to keep it right
Fulfilling all obligations of love making tonight
Lovers 4 life should be the night's soundtrack, as it is so fitting
Paradise found in your hidden treasure
As I dive deep into this sexual utopia, let's love
Understanding is the key
Relaxation happens to be your comfortable seduction
When did you come, to this point
I've came, to accept, we are love
Did I go too deep
Did this truth hurt because I have a lifetime of more love to share
Open your eyes and come with me
Let worry and all other inhibition saturate the sheets as you put it on me
                                        Lovers 4 life I pray we will be

INVISIBLE KISSES

Let your imagination guide these invisible kisses
As they journey miles to their sweet destination
Arriving at the most pleasurable places
Now feel the fingerprints of seduction leaving lasting sensation in abundance
Scaling the walls of your inhibitions
No need to be suspicious
Have faith in your intuition
I come bearing gifts
Gifts of compassion, faithfulness, love
Divinely routed in respect
So with all that is due, baby I long for you
Your physique is a masterpiece
A masterpiece to be unveiled by the hands of passion
The vision is vivid
Stimulating all five senses
Your voice whispers echoes of tranquility elevating my desire to taste your serenity
Chocolate ecstasy
And as your sweet escape begins to melt due to the extreme heat
You find yourself in the realms of pleasuredom
This is a place you have to come
Over, and over, and over
Where invisible kisses manifest into something everlasting
Something real
Something true
Something only understood by me and you

LOST LOVERS

Questions are answered
Seconds are saved
Minutes are wasted
Emotions are enslaved
Take a mental walk with me
Like Jill Scott
Let my mind be your sweet fruit good to the last drop
Lets not look too deep into an abyss but focus on the penetrating present
As it feels so pleasant
Like the findings of hidden treasure to a peasant
Subliminal emotions so divine as if we're really controlling time
What do we profit from an atmosphere so relaxed and elegant
When our present reality is so irrelevant
He had you confused so you looked to me for answers
Serious as cancer
Body of a dancer
Face of a goddess
Wrong seeds bad harvest
As we become hungry animals in the realms of our own hidden world
Appetite for destruction as I lick your fingers
One's moves are bold when one has a heart of stone
What I'm saying is that your pains were once mine
My girl, you call me your boy
A fool's heart is destined to be destroyed, diminished, devastated, and finished
It's senseless
One long last kiss goodnight as we misdirect the inevitable, and end this

AS I ANSWER MY QUESTIONS

The very first time I heard your voice
That's when I made the choice
The choice to always want to hear the same
To always want to hear you speak my name
Because I saw your truth in your eyes
That's why I promised to never lie
Being without you has almost become a sin in my religion of love
But where space is needed space is given
That's why this space will be used for mistakes forgiven
I listen and pay attention therefore I give you a premonition of a clear vision
Yes I kissed your lips and discovered your sweet serenity
That's why my threshold for passion is unlimited
Uninhibited raw human need is the reason why I'm not afraid to dream
Your face never fades away from my memory bank
It's clear as day
Beauty unmatched
Potential untapped
Limitless love unlatched
This is why I refuse to let love die
Because of you that's who
All things in the world must bare your stamp of approval to be called beautiful
Why wouldn't I put my cards on the table face up
Flawless to me without the enhancements of makeup
Dream that wonderful dream baby doll, why force the wakeup
Everything in our universe has its season
Who was it, it was you that gave me the reason to keep believing
Holding you in my arms reinforces the strength I want to share with you
The pain I want to bare for you
The deepest and truest of ways that I care for you
Your love is like the sea, let me ride your waves
Guide me through the storm with your lighthouse of shelter, companionship, and better days
So what is it all about
It's about you making me love you without trying
It's about you giving birth to my resurrection without me dying
It's about me tasting your tears
It's about me helping you chase away your fears
Who is it about
It's about you
Why
Because it can't be about anyone else
When
Forever plus time served
Where

In a space called "Free 2 Be Loved"
What I'm trying to say is this
We love each other, need each other, and nowhere in the world is there a better fix

LOVE IS THE CONCLUSION

Your voice
Your smile
Your style
God told me to be patient
So how far away is heaven
I feel free now
I want you to be with me now
My completeness is through you
Complete me is what you do
If this world were mine
You would no longer have to worry
If I controlled the time you would no longer have to rush
When you touch me I feel it in my soul
From my soul I give you love
Real love
Not the illusion
I hope you understand my conclusion

THAT COMEBACK

What is the meaning of this new feeling
I can't stand it but I love it
An out of body experience as I penetrate your premises
Persevere through your parameter
Break down all walls
Rebirth you into the new
When love calls this is what lovers do
Invade your underground hole
Take it over, plant my flag pole
Milk and chocolate, mattress, wall, and carpet
Ecstasy Land Magical Ride, you hate to get off it
Stacked like a thoroughbred
Give thorough head
Don't be misled
We're in the same chapter, same page, same road, same word
Highway 69, same curves
Unique from head to feet
Sweet
The lust is captured
No surrender no retreat
Just subtle back scratches
Hot climaxes
Grind game in harmony with the resistance of the mattress
As I pick the lock to your palace
Dive deep for the gold, warm waters never cold
Every second is a minute
Every minute is an hour
Every hour is a day so everyday we meet is ours
Backyard to the shower
Pollination of your flower
Lakefront, break-lunch
Boring lovers hate us
Hilltop, sunset, cool breeze, much sweat
Sexy southern belle with a well chiseled roughneck
Keep it all in context
Damn girl we just met
It is what it is boo and I ain't had enough yet
That's that comeback

WHAT WOULD LOVE DO

Would love take me to the edge of the earth
Does love hurt
When I fall in love first why does it never work
I learned that real love is only heaven sent
So I pray everyday for some evidence
Is love a two-way street
Should I get on it and ride
Why do some want to hide if it feels so nice
Love is only a word
That's what I heard from some non-believers
While they're teaching us to love racist leaders
So I'm twisted in the pastime
Spreading pure love and now they want to ban mine
The other side of love
Angelic queens giving birth to future kings
Let the words of righteous leaders reign
Is this love

A WORD FOR THE STREETS

Stop pulling me down
You've never seen my face
Or have you
Do you work hand in hand with the man
Your endless desires to admire lazy liars
That's kind of tired
I'm still searching for an end though
Is there one
Everywhere I wander you find me
Holding me down
Magnetic to energetic athletic
My words mean a thing
My actions cause satisfaction
Inches away from blaming it on your distractions
Remember the time
Nah forget it
Let's live in the vivid
Savor the moment
It's most irrelevant that my love is my opponent
Is it really
The teary eye belongs to me
Because of the heat
Delivered by these streets

SUCCESS IS IN THE RIVER

As people we go with the flow
Flow with the current
I've learned to keep my head up through the roughest of times
Handling the tides
Skimming the surface
Going with the flow
So many faces and unforeseen places
Dive deep young wise
Learn and don't be afraid
Go with the seasoned diver
Seek and ye shall find
Go away with the trailblazers of truth and righteousness
No child left behind
You will have what you need
I guarantee
I've been on the floor
I've searched with those who have not
I've shared with those who need most
I'm able to keep my eyes open and breathe with deep breaths
I searched way down deep and found what I call success

UNTIL NEXT TIME

I've never shed a tear of joy in my life
They were all bitter, most even sour
My minutes are hours
Here, take some of this pain as all my love is shared in vain
My smiles are not the same as they once were
Stretched out by the illusion of pure happiness
If all existence was centered in my substance, the world woud be boring
Therefore I won't complain
Let me be misunderstood
From the tone of my jokes to the depths of my hope
I've come to conquer all fears so I take everything in stride now
Nothing to hide now
Would a lie from eye seem more believable since my truths fall on deaf ears, closed minds, and cold hearts
Should I isolate myself and dream alone
Call myself on my own phone and discuss where I went wrong
It hasn't paid off yet
I'm tired of putting my heart in a song
I'm hurt due to my own partaking
Trying to do right only brings me cold sweats and rude awakenings
Heartaches and backslides
The universe is gangster the way it watches over this stranger
Forgiveness for my anger
All I can do is put my god first
My queen got me back in church
I love the balance of a woman
Her wrath is as whole as her warmth
The look in her eyes is as deep as the revenge in her mind
I wear this mirage proudly
I was lost until love found me
Seek God and you will only find yourself
Seek yourself and you will only find God
Look after and over me Lord
My foolish ways have turned the corner on me again
Living and learning for we were all born in sin
I love like I fight
Till death
See this is all I have left
Hate is a wasted emotion, fear is also
If heaven was a mile away, follow me, we'll all go
The heart of a king beating out of my torso
Can't make up lost ground
Too far to turn around
Footprints burned in the ground while the present is fertile ground

Next chapter
New page
Pack luck and caution while traveling this trail I blazed
The print of my face is in the clouds
Let's stare at each other in hopes of feeling better
Feet planted firmly in the sand
Ready for whatever
Positive energy never dies
Even through Blizzards in the Desert

ABOUT THE AUTHOR

The common thread Donald Charles has throughout this body of work is love. Donald Charles is a poet and hip-hop artist that goes by the performance name of Dukki Boi(pronounced Ducky Boy). Born and raised in New Orleans, Louisiana, Donald has been writing poetry and hip-hop music since his early days of high school. In an attempt to captivate and capture the hearts and minds of everyone who reads this book, Donald pours an ocean of thoughts and emotions into every poem.

Made in the USA
Columbia, SC
12 March 2025